*A portion of the proceeds will be donated
to research and development toward
cystic fibrosis and finding a cure.*

DISCOVER YOUR BEST SELF ... AND STICK WITH IT!

A GUIDE TO CREATING A WINNING IMAGE

CHRISTINE FOWLER-PHILLIPS

Archway Publishing books may be ordered through booksellers or by contacting:

Archway Publishing
1663 Liberty Drive
Bloomington, IN 47403
www.archwaypublishing.com
1 (888) 242-5904

Because of the dynamic nature of the Internet, any web addresses or links contained in this book may have changed since publication and may no longer be valid. The views expressed in this work are solely those of the author and do not necessarily reflect the views of the publisher, and the publisher hereby disclaims any responsibility for them.

Any people depicted in stock imagery provided by Getty Images are models, and such images are being used for illustrative purposes only. Certain stock imagery © Getty Images.

ISBN: 978-1-4808-6409-2 (sc)
ISBN: 978-1-4808-6410-8 (e)

Library of Congress Control Number: 2018947879

Print information available on the last page.

Archway Publishing rev. date: 10/10/2018

CONTENTS

DEDICATION

I dedicate this book to God for without him I would have never discovered my "best self." I am grateful for his wisdom and divine order. He keeps me focused on what really matters in life. Also, thank you to my phenomenal husband Terrance for being the wind beneath my wings and to my amazing and beautiful daughter Madisyn for always supporting and believing in Mommy. Thank you both for your unwavering support and unconditional love.

This book is a labor of passion, envisioned and created from my desire to help others find their true selves. I hope the destinies of many will be fulfilled with the help of my encouragement and my suggestions and not hindered by a lack of confidence in their own God- given talents or their ability to put their best self forward.

Lastly, to those loved ones "gone too soon," all of whom truly had a major impact on my life and are a major reason why, at a very young age I was encouraged to discover my "best self," I thank you for your role in my life. My mother Jane English, my father Benjamin Fowler, my Godmother/Aunt Mattie English, and last but certainly not least my beloved brother, Anthony Fowler Sr., were all a great part of my motivation. My gratitude runs deep as I reflect on all of my blessings!

FOREWORD

Discover Your Best Self … And Stick with It, A Guide to Creating a Winning Image is a self-help book gently reminding us to stay on the path of self-discovery. I'm honored to write this foreword in support of my friend, Christine Fowler-Phillips. I am confident that her words of wisdom will help others.

The author and I were introduced by a mutual friend and her strength and confidence were evident immediately. I could tell she was a fortress; flawless from head to toe, Christine is a walking visual of what she encourages her readers to aspire to become. As our friendship developed I learned more about her warrior spirit and fierce determination to help others. She has been an advocate for HIV/AIDS and Cystic Fibrosis for many years and is committed to community service.

Discover Your Best Self offers a clear path to reclaim your identity when life throws you a curve-ball. That's what happened to me. As an EMMY nominated reporter for a New York City television station and seen daily by millions of viewers, I need to bring my "A-game" to the job every day. This became an immense struggle after I lost my husband, the love of my life, at the height of our lives together. His death, which came one month after our third miscarriage, broke my spirit. It was then that I realized that my 'Best Self' in my 40's was not going to resemble what it had been in my 20's and 30's. I needed to find another approach to defining and discovering a new me.

Discovering your best self is a continual process that changes with life's circumstances. This book shows us the discovery is always just a few thought processes away. Through the implementation of the skill sets discussed by the author, I am encouraged to keep moving in the direction that is right for me. She encourages us to be confident and to always put forth our best in everything we do.

Self-reflection, internal motivation, self-empowerment and emotional intelligence are what Christine emphasizes as "key elements" and are the character traits she saw in me as I tackled life head-on. Practicing what she teaches, Christine constantly re-invents herself and proudly acknowledges that she will be discovering her "Best Self" for the rest of her life.

I encourage you to read this book, heed her advice and incorporate its principles as you strive *to "Discover Your Best Self ... and Stick with it!"*

Darla Miles

News Reporter, WABC-TV New York

PREFACE

As far back as I can remember I've always looked up to those whom I felt embodied positivity, spirituality and confidence. They, to me, alluded a total package of everything that I found important and their appearance and character suggested they were presenting their "Best Self" at all times.

Academy Award winner and one of my all-time favorite entertainers and actresses, Ms. Diahann Carroll, is someone who I've admired for years because I always felt that she depicted strength, confidence and intelligence. She was always in control. I cannot recall ever watching her in a role that portrayed anything but strength and confidence.

When I was just a four-year-old little girl, my older brother would always dress me up in pretty outfits that made me feel extra special. He would take my picture and develop them in his personal photo-lab where he created many family images and memories. I cannot say this was the sole factor that ignited my inner conscientiousness making me want to always put my best foot forward, however, it is probably my earliest memory of seeing myself "at my best." As I grew up, this theme became a part of who I would become. It had been ingrained to always make sure that my outward appearance and my inward spirit were ready to meet whomever I encountered. Being prepared and ready was a reputation that would stick with me throughout my high school, college and professional career.

I wrote this book because I wanted to put everything that I've heard and learned throughout my life into a guide that I hope will help anyone looking to improve their chances for success regardless of their circumstances or any obstacles they may face. This book is about *Discovering Your Best Self* so that you can be prepared to tackle life's challenges. I thank my brother Roger Fowler Sr., for constantly encouraging me to put *Discovering Your Best Self* in print.

INTRODUCTION

We've all heard the phrase "Image is everything." I believe that image is developed from the inside and enhanced by our outward presentation. By that, I mean that how we feel inwardly is usually projected and reflected outwardly. If we feel great about ourselves, we will want to present our best outward appearance. This book is divided into two sections to discuss both Inward and Outward Images.

Many of us live our lives searching for the formula to success. We often find ourselves looking at others who we feel embody success and think we can copy their blueprint. Success to you could be the 3-time Academy Award winner, the 4-time Super Bowl MVP, or the Citizen of the Year for your local community organization, as success can be identified or defined in many ways. What I have found is that we each have our own set of expectations as to what success looks like. What seems like success to one may not be what defines success to others.

The book is to help direct you in *Discovering Your Best Self* so that you will bring your A-game every single day to achieve the success that you want. Doing this will give you the best chance to accomplish all that you desire in life. Your goal should be to let those around you see you at the top of your game, regardless of the environment that you're in, and never allowing yourself to be deterred by negative circumstances, which could inhibit your growth. Always have the confidence that you can achieve your objectives regardless of the barriers that are placed in your path. It is also important to use basic tools including etiquette and manners to encourage a positive perception of yourself to others and help you as you navigate your career path.

I've traveled to many places, have met many people, and have been exposed to a variety of cultures thus far in my life. I've noticed inconsistency in how people present themselves. One day someone looks like a million dollars, the next day they look like one dollar. I've seen someone give the most motivating speech at one venue, yet give a boring presentation at another. *Discovering Your Best Self* means identifying the formula that allows you to be at the top of your game in every facet of your life all the time, every time. It means finding the source of motivation that will encourage you to stay sharp and relevant in any environment. We only have one chance to live our lives and achieve the success that we all want and desire. Life, it's said, "Is not a dress rehearsal." Identifying our best selves gives us the chance to reach heights that some only dare to dream about. Don't dream. Do.

As you read the different sections of this book, think about the tips and suggestions I provide. Evaluate what has worked for you in the past to accomplish a major or minor achievement. Use this book as a guide to establishing a winning image. I don't want you to think that this book will guarantee your success in life; nothing can do that except your own conscious efforts. The prerequisite to the most satisfying careers, family lives, and great health is hard work. There are no short cuts to being the best of the best.

While I believe in working smart, it doesn't necessarily mean that the smartest solutions are the easiest roads to success but what we labor for today will provide dividends tomorrow. Case in point: more often than not the quality time we spend in the gym working to lose weight or maintain a healthy life style will in fact enable us to live longer and healthier lives. On the job, the time you put into preparing for a presentation, (that you hope will win you the contract or promotion that ultimately changes the game for you or your company), will be well worth the rewards and recognition that come after.

As we work towards discovering our best selves, it is also imperative that we understand that bringing a positive mental state to our game plan is essential. In Part II, Inner Image, I will discuss self-awareness and self-reflection, skill sets that are extremely important.

Emotional Intelligence, understanding your emotional self, will also be explained. Accepting who you are naturally and your genetic makeup, along with what you have learned from your environment, and knowing how to channel your positive energy is very important in being well rounded. It takes discipline and more to be able to create a plan that will get you to the finish line and take you beyond.

Find the formula that makes you the best in all that you are and all that you do and stick with it!

PART I

Outward Image

Outward image is comprised of your physical appearance and your public image. It is a representation of who you are. This image is a mirror of the parts of your behavior that you put on display. It is how others know you, and it creates a general impression of yourself that you present to the public.

I'm sure you've heard the proverb "first impressions are the most lasting impressions." Everyone talks about the power of first impressions, so this important section of the book sets the foundation for you to realize the value of exhibiting your best outward image.

If you think about it, we all want to leave a positive opinion with everyone we meet, be it social or professional—especially on job interviews. We try to look our best and impress when we are meeting a new friend, employer, family member, or anyone for the first time. I encourage you to go out of your way to make an outstanding first impression. Experts say that we size up new people in the first thirty seconds to two minutes of meeting them. That isn't much time, especially when you are interviewing, so it's important to put forth your best effort consistently. No one wants to walk away from an encounter thinking that they failed to do all they could have done to enhance their image and reputation. A good rule of thumb when interviewing is: "Dress for the job you want, *not* for the job you have," and in general: "Dress to impress."

Using that as a point of reference can help us in our daily preparation for work and play. When preparing for the workplace, always dress with the mindset that you are ready for any unexpected event. Sometimes there are impromptu meetings with senior management that occur at the drop of a dime and might require your immediate visible and verbal participation on an important matter.

No one intends to show up to a meeting unprepared on a subject or likes to find herself underdressed for the situation. Your superiors and co-workers will form an instant impression of you based on your body language, mannerisms, and demeanor, in addition to how you are dressed. Think about how humiliating it would be if your attire were inappropriate.

Question yourself. Are you ready to be seen and heard? Are you confident that your appearance is on point? How will your public image be impacted? Think about consequences. Failure to prepare is to prepare to fail.

Sure, I agree that what you articulate verbally should ultimately be the most important contribution you make at any meeting, but oftentimes it is not. People can be very judgmental based on your appearance, so present your best self at all times.

I'm a proponent of always looking my best regardless of where I'm headed. People tell me that I look like I'm going somewhere special when I am just stepping out to the supermarket. Even if it's a trip to the bus stop to pick up my teenage daughter, I always make sure that I am presentable to anyone I may encounter. What's "presentable"? You decide that for yourself. I encourage you to feel self-assured in how you are dressed and to always be cognizant of the fact that you never know who you may meet or where you may end up when you leave your house.

I think that it's important to always be prepared for the unexpected. I recall a time when a local newspaper reporter stopped my husband and our daughter outside of a supermarket. They were asked about disaster preparation in light of bad weather predictions. Obviously, they didn't leave home expecting to be approached by someone from the local media (who, by the way, had a cameraperson ready to capture a shot of the interview). Fortunately, they were both dressed presentable, and the newspaper photo was acceptable to both the mommy and wife in me!

While such an occurrence will most likely not happen to you on the average trip to the store, the point is that you never want to be in a situation where your appearance does not truly embody you. It doesn't have to be your best look … but it should be a look you will be proud of after the fact.

With the importance of outward appearance defined and its necessity stressed, let's now discuss image and etiquette in relation to the corporate world.

Corporate Etiquette

Etiquette refers to having good manners and having polite behavior in public or among members of your profession or group. Today, there are so many environments where our etiquette plays a part in how we are perceived by others. I could write an entire book on this subject alone and on situations where lacking the customary polite behavior equates to social suicide. One must make a conscious effort to learn and practice correct etiquette.

With the explosion of social media, something you say or how you appear can quickly go viral. Thus, a few tips on etiquette in personal and professional settings will go a long way in helping you to maintain a positive image.

Here are what I identify to be the best practices to demonstrate good etiquette in your workplace:

- Always wear professional attire. You never want your clothing to tell a story that paints you in a negative light. It is important to avoid clothing that is not flattering to your body type. Instead, dress appropriately for your weight and height.

- Keep yourself well groomed and maintain good hygiene. Keep your hair clean and in a style that is appropriate for the work environment. Keep nails clean and nicely manicured. Keep your piercings and tattoo art in less conspicuous areas to prevent prejudice and misconceptions about your personality and work ethic.

- Avoid discussions on politics and religion. There are usually no winners in those talks, and discussing these topics can often lead to negative opinions and disagreements. Discussing your political affiliation and religious practices are best left outside the workplace. Even if you work with friends and family, you should still stay clear of discussions of this nature.

- Avoid office politics. Office politics happen in just about every organization. You will encounter those on the job who use strategies and influence to gain or retain power; this is a form of politics as they try to garner support for their own advancement. Try to stay clear of conversations that are based on speculation and rumors. You should maintain neutrality when exposed to information that may be personal in nature as it relates to a colleague or peer.

- Put your cellular telephone and mobile alerts on silent. No one wants to hear your favorite song on your ringtone when you're at work. Imagine a situation where an ill-timed audio blast from your mobile device goes off in the middle of a meeting. That will definitely not be a good look. Keep those devices on vibrate. There is a time and a place for everything.

- Practice being punctual consistently. Showing up late to an important meeting is never acceptable. Do not assume that others will wait for you to arrive. Have respect for specified time frames set by those organizing the events you attend. There is a reason why organizations set starting times. Often the first few minutes of a meeting are when important points, goals, and objectives are mentioned, and you are expected to be there. Being on time or early gives you the best opportunity to stay ahead of the game. You don't want to be labeled as unorganized or lackadaisical because of your consistent tardiness to key events.

- Allow yourself more than enough time to go where you need to be or to arrive at the specified location to ensure that you aren't the "Johnny come lately" knocking on the door after the meeting starts.

- Avoid involving yourself in the business of others. Eavesdropping or answering someone's telephone in their absence should never occur unless they explicitly give you permission to do so on their behalf. These actions are a clear violation of privacy and are an etiquette no-no. Never press for information that wasn't shared with you. If you feel that information has been withheld and that perhaps it should have been shared, you need to exercise discretion and diplomacy when you address this issue. When discussing a specific problem or concern, make sure to also have a reasonable resolution.

- When you are sick, do yourself and your co-workers a favor ... stay home! Unless the company will collapse in your absence, which is highly unlikely, you are doing yourself and your co-workers a disservice by coming into work sick. You not only risk contaminating others, but you are not giving yourself an opportunity to heal when you trek into work too soon.

- Maintain a clean workspace. Whether you have an office or a cubicle, be sure to keep your work environment clean. A cluttered desk is often seen as the mark of a disorganized person. You do not want that perception in the workplace as it may prevent you from being promoted or considered for high-impact projects or assignments.

- Always answer a call in a timely manner. I am not just referring to telephone calls. I am also referring to those times when you are asked to provide assistance, guidance, or help with a project. Employees who take too long to address simple tasks are often judged negatively. Do not adopt a casual, nonchalant attitude. Take your job seriously; your company expects you to perform your duties as required. Do not disappoint them. Be willing, ready, and able.

- Park in the space assigned to you. Do not park in areas designated for specific employees or for other purposes. More and more companies today are creating assigned parking spaces for hybrid cars or cars that use electricity. Do not inconvenience anyone that may need that spot for its intended purpose. Definitely do not park in a handicapped space if you are not entitled to do so.

- Never drink alcoholic beverages at work. Keep your alcohol consumption to a minimum when attending company functions where drinking is allowed. It is so easy for one drink to lead to several drinks. What you do and how much you consume in your private time should always be tailored when you are out with co-workers at a company-sponsored event.

Interview Etiquette

A firm handshake when you meet a potential employer is a must. It presents a strong, positive impression and sends a signal of confidence from the beginning. Smile! A great smile shows sincerity and that you are genuinely happy to meet the person. There's a saying, "Smile and the world smiles too." Be polite, courteous and friendly but keep it as a demonstration of your true authentic self and don't overdo it.

During the interview, be sure to listen and be prepared to ask questions. Smart questions, not just small talk. Asking good questions shows that you are listening to the job requirements and expectations and that you are interested in knowing why or how a process works.

Usually your resume has been electronically submitted before you go on an interview, but it doesn't hurt to have hard copies just in case the interviewer asks and it's always good to have a list of references with phone numbers that you can leave behind.

Should you meet a prospective employer over lunch or dinner remember your table manners because dining with clients could become a part of your job and potential employers are watching your dining etiquette skills as well as your social skills.

Make eye contact with everyone at the table. Engage in light chitchat sprinkled with questions pertaining to the job.

Be considerate; don't order the most expensive thing on the menu, nor the messiest foods. Don't talk with your mouth full of food. Take small bites so that you can swallow quickly to answer questions. Just as in company social hours, do not over drink. It might be best not to drink alcohol at this meal unless it would be socially awkward because everyone else is having a glass of wine or liquor. If you are a non-drinker, it is ok to say so and refrain.

At the end of the meeting, ask when you might hear something about the next steps in the hiring process and graciously thank your interviewer for their time.

Lastly, avoid an awkward situation and allow the prospective employer to pick up the tab since he or she has invited you and expects to do so.

Manners

Corporate etiquette is the perfect segue into a discussion on manners. Manners are how you behave towards other people; they are your actions. You hear of someone being referred to as "having the manner of a gentleman," meaning his actions of being polite or courteous were noticed. Perhaps you have heard someone say, "She is behaving like a lady." Again, it means her actions or manners are being noticed. So, let's touch on some basic actions that will demonstrate that we are bringing our A-game into the corporate environment.

- Always hold the door for those who may be entering behind you. This seems like an obvious courtesy, but you would be shocked by the amount of times that I've seen people allow the door to close on those coming in behind them. All it takes is courtesy and consideration on your part. The effort is minimal to nothing for performing this kind gesture.

- Offer your seat to someone who may need it more than you. Men usually offer their seats to ladies and the elderly. Ladies at times even offer their seat to other ladies who are pregnant or handicapped. It is a sign of common courtesy to offer your seat to someone and signifies respect and politeness.

- Respond to invitations. When a letter or invitation states "Please RSVP," you must respond to let the person know whether or not you can attend the event. This is a French phrase, "repondez, s'il vous plait," which means please reply and is a polite request from the sender. Anyone who receives an invitation with RSVP should do so in a prompt and timely manner. As an invited guest, you should reply indicating whether you will attend or will not be attending. A response is required in either situation. To not respond is rude. The expression "Regrets only" is used for occasions where it isn't necessary to respond that you will attend, the host will assume you are coming and is asking only for notice that you will not be attending. RSVP: Reply, I will or I will not attend. Regrets only: Reply, I will not be attending. Easy, right?

- When dining allow others to choose a place at the table first. Always place your napkin in your lap immediately. At some very fancy restaurants the waiter may do this for you but it is always appropriate for you to do it for yourself. Things you surely know, but may have forgotten:

- Avoid shaking your napkin open.

- Avoid cleaning the cutlery or wiping your face with the napkin.

- Avoid using the napkin to wipe your nose.

When there are 6 or fewer at the table you should wait to eat until everyone is served. At a private dinner party wait until your host or hostess picks up their fork to eat and then you may eat. If your host or hostess insists that you start eating immediately, you can do so.

Using your utensils: Start from the outside and work your way in. This means using the silverware farthest from your plate first. Regarding which dinnerware belongs to you, the rule is eat to your left, drink to your right. Any food dish to the left is yours, (bread or dessert plates) and any glasses to the right are yours (water or wine).

There are also rules regarding a hostess gift that should be mentioned as a part of dining etiquette outside the workplace. It is proper to bring a small hostess gift but not one that the hostess feels obliged to put out during the evening. Flowers, candy, wine or dessert are not good hostess gifts, as the hostess will feel compelled to share it. Do not take a gift expecting to partake in it. Lastly, a thank you note should be sent to your hostess after a formal dinner party. If you know your hostess well, a phone call is also acceptable.

Professional, Business Casual, And Dress-Down Attire

Many companies offer their employees the option to choose between professional business and casual business attire, and some often allow very casual attire on days referred to as a "dress-down" day. The rules for all acceptable dress are often communicated by your company's Human Resources Department and will include a list of do's and don'ts.

The problem is that there are those who will either ignore the company guidelines, which is problematic; or do not clearly understand the difference between casual clothing and dress-down clothes, and then there are those who simply do not know how to dress appropriately for the workplace no matter what the dress code is. I will provide clarity for, surprisingly, what many struggle to understand.

I will also introduce and discuss the concept of branding. Branding is how companies or employees integrate corporate image into their own style or brand. First, let's discuss how to differentiate professional business attire from business casual dress and from dress- down attire. I will explain what each is and what is appropriate when.

Professional Attire

Generally, a great rule of thumb is to follow what I call the Interview Rule. This rule implies that if you would wear it to an interview then it is considered professional business attire. If you are having trouble determining what you would wear to an interview, then here is a short list of suggestions.

1. Men should wear a conservative dress suit and tie. Women wear conservative dress suits with either a skirt or pants or wear a dress that is considered business style.

2. Don't dress how you envision or have seen company employees dress. You are not yet an employee.

3. Don't overdress or underdress. If you could navigate your way through the parking lot or through the building without unnecessary attention then it is probably proper attire. On the contrary, if you are drawing whistles, catcalls or stares, perhaps you are not in professional clothing and should reconsider your choice.

4. Stick to basics. Black, gray or navy works well for men and ladies. Colorful and lively clothing is not for the interview.

Keep in mind these are just guides to help demonstrate proper interview attire. Think in terms of quality instead of quantity. One simple bracelet is better than an armful of bangles or wearing rings on every finger. A classic leather portfolio is better than a backpack or loud colorful bag.

There was a time when a suit was the only way to show up for an interview and although times have changed, sticking to that standard won't hurt. Once you've landed the job, you may still want to follow the standard if your company is conservative.

Business Casual

Always let the corporate culture of the company be your guide. The important thing is to dress appropriately for your workspace. As you become more comfortable with your company's culture you may be able to deviate from ultra-conservative professional attire to more casual business attire.

While business casual is an ambiguously defined dress code, it is usually a classic, clean, professional look. No athletic wear. It is always best to inquire about the dress code because you could have interviewed on a "dress down day" (description to follow) and what you observed is not the standard expected dress.

Business casual is, for example, that men may now omit the tie but still wear collared, long-sleeved button down shirts with or without a jacket. They may also wear polo shirts or knit shirts with a collar and casual crew neck sweaters along with khaki pants. Ladies may wear pantsuits with blouses or sweaters. Business casual clothing is just a level below formal professional clothing. Think of it in "Dress for Success" terms. Colors remain basic neutral shades of black, gray and navy but may include white and off white. Now, let's discuss what constitutes dress-down attire.

Determining Proper Dress-Down Attire

A company may offer their employees the option of wearing business casual attire on a daily basis (which as previously stated means appropriate, professional and clean) with no requirements of a tie and as a privilege they may also allow for a weekly dress-down day.

The challenge with an attire protocol with that kind of flexibility in corporate settings is when some employees cross the line between business casual and dress down. As noted earlier, The Human Resources (HR) Department typically defines standard and appropriate wardrobe with specific guidelines about what is acceptable and what is not. Following those guides should be your first line of defense.

In the absence of HR mandated guidelines, keep the following in mind as you gear up for days that are designated as dress-down.

Always be mindful of wearing anything too revealing. For men, keep your shirts buttoned up to an appropriate height. No chest hair on display! No one needs to see that you might be related to the Wolf Man.

Jeans are usually fine. You should avoid ripped jeans with holes though and this rule goes for both genders. T-shirts are usually not acceptable in most business settings but today more and more companies, especially those in social media arenas or tech boom companies, are becoming more liberal with t-shirts. My advice? I would still play it safe and wear a collared shirt even on dress-down days. Sales, fashion, and social media companies are definitely more open to piercings and tattoos and what I call "non-conventional" work clothes.

What about body art, piercings? Given the enormous change in our culture and cosmetic trends over the years, these are not as taboo as before. Err on the side of caution, especially if you work in a traditionally conservative industry like banking or financial services; keep the body art covered.

As a rule use the dress-down concept to make your workday more comfortable and enjoyable. Avoid coming to work in something that you would wear around the house on the weekend. The environment at work and at home are totally different and there's a chance you might leave an unfavorable impression on co-workers or others you spend the majority of your work day with if you fail to heed these suggestions.

Next, let's examine wardrobe mistakes to avoid not only in corporate America but in general as well; better known as … Fashion Faux Pas.

Fashion Faux Pas

Here is a list of wardrobe red flags you want to be conscious of as you discover your best self:

- Wearing clothes too small or tight.

- Wearing evening makeup during the day.

- Wearing see through clothing.

- Wearing a hat to an interview.

- Using excessive perfume or cologne.

Choosing Your Wardrobe

Many of us walk into a department store and see clothing that fits perfectly on the display models yet when we try on the same clothing we are often disappointed. Attempting to force a look or style is never a good thing as it may not be the right style for you. You may not have the right body type for the clothes you are trying to fit into. Skinny jeans are not for everyone!

Learning what looks best on you may take getting feedback from others who are around you often. Sometimes we can't see ourselves like others see us. We may want to dress like a movie star or professional athlete but their clothing choices may not be appropriate for our body type or accessible for our budgets.

The clothing we see on celebrities and athletes are usually custom tailored to fit them. They are meant to look like "walking perfection" and the public expects a certain standard of showmanship from its celebrities and public figures. With that said, what you should do is find a local tailor who can help you get a proper fit by tailoring your clothes to look as though they were designed specifically for you.

Learning where to shop and knowing what clothing looks good on you will go a long way in helping you reveal your best self. Today, shopping online offers us a lot of options and requires less effort than going out to retail stores. Online shopping appeals to many but what looks good online or on television may not necessarily look the same once you buy it and it arrives at your home. For this reason, a good rule of thumb to which I subscribe is to shop in places where you can try the clothes on before you purchase.

If your preference is to purchase your clothing online then you should be familiar with the designer's cut and size chart. If you know how their clothing is tailored, you can determine proper sizing and what is a good choice for you. Should you buy something online that doesn't fit properly, or doesn't appear as advertised or as "seen on TV," don't worry, use that tailor I spoke of who can do the alterations and help you accomplish your look.

Knowing what colors look best on you is another essential aspect to finding the most appropriate clothing and building a flattering wardrobe. Having a color analysis done, which is the process of finding colors to match ones skin complexion, eye color, and hair color could be of enormous help as you shop. Ultimately you want clothing and make-up that will complement your complexion. Try to stay away from colors that will be too stark in contrast to your own color tone (too bright, too dark, etc.). You want colors that will enhance your skin tone.

Once you understand what looks best on you, you should consider your audience or the environment where you will be. You don't want to dress like you are going to cocktail party if you are going to an interview. Conversely, you don't want to dress as if you're going on an interview if you are going to a festive, holiday office party. There is clearly a time and place when certain attire is most appropriate.

The thing to do is to discover what looks best on you and stick with that look. This involves knowing what clothing is most complementary to you, your body type, personality, and the environment.

Posture

As a Corporate Image Consultant I spend a lot of time discussing the importance of posture, walking, and communication. I consider these three topics to be among the most important factors in establishing a positive image.

Your body posture says a lot about you but many people don't realize that. Your posture gives others a perception of you … whether it is positive or negative.

What is good posture? Hold your head up, your shoulders back, and look straight ahead. Seems pretty simple doesn't it? If it comes naturally to you, it is easy, but If you have developed bad posture habits throughout your life it can require practice to undo those.

Changing our posture is difficult because how we walk, our gait and our stride were developed perhaps as early as when we took our first steps and for years we have walked in that same manner. Old habits are hard to break.

People pay attention to your posture and body language. If you tend to slouch or slump over when you walk, there's a good chance that someone will read or interpret that as a lack of confidence. On the other hand, if you walk with your head up and shoulders back, this may be noticed in a much more positive light.

I encourage everyone to walk with a purpose. What do I mean? Essentially, walk with self-assurance and conviction. A strong physical representation is the best way to display poise and assertiveness. On the contrary, disabilities aside, those who walk watching the ground, humped or slouched over convey just the opposite.

Does walking with conviction mean strutting around like a peacock and drawing lots of attention? No. Will a strong, purposeful walk automatically give you confidence in the boardroom or at that next interview? Of course not. But it will help you feel more confident and you can continue to work on the other areas that build self-assurance. By the way, there is nothing wrong with having a little swag in your step.

Branding

Personal Branding

Personal branding means establishing something unique to your own style that allows people to remember you. Whether it's a certain hairstyle, or type of shoe, clothing or the way you greet someone, your personal brand is what people associate with you when they think of you. Well known actor and entertainer Will Smith has branded himself with his quirky humor and his trademark goatee. Lady Gaga branded herself with her outrageous outfits and unique and entertaining music.

Athletes are known to also brand themselves beyond the products that they endorse. It's not uncommon to see professional basketball players with a plethora of unique tattoo's that become their brand. Those are a few examples of what individuals do to brand themselves.

Your personal brand is more than a trademark; rather, it is what is etched in people's minds when your name is mentioned. What do you want people to think of when they think about you? Many times we brand ourselves without knowing it. This can be done by our personal actions and mannerisms. This is why we also should be conscious of how we present ourselves in public. We want to provide the most positive image or brand that others will come to associate with us.

Corporate Brand

Corporate branding is the promotion of a brand name as opposed to specific products or services. A company's brand is *Who* they are, *What* they do, *Why* they do it and *Who* they do it for. It is essentially a pledge of consistency that consumers come to expect from that brand name. The company logo is what consumers visually see and usually rely on when evaluating a new product.

When a new product is released, if it is attached to a well-established company it gives it a higher credibility. The ultimate achievement for a corporation is to have a brand that is so strong that it can be identified by a logo alone. We all recognize the "Golden Arches," the athletic "Swoosh," and the apple with the bite mark and know what to expect when we see it.

It is important for today's companies to ensure that their branding aligns with company culture. Culture is the social behavior found in human societies; how they dress, perceive things, and interact with one another. The branding process starts way before someone is hired for the company. Those who are tasked with recruiting and training new hires should be able to articulate in writing and verbal communication the company's brand. The company logo, brand, and vision statement should be visible as a constant reminder to employees.

Recruiters and trainers share the responsibility of educating employees on the importance of understanding the goals and vision set forth by the leadership in the company. Line managers have a great deal of responsibilities when they take on new employees. Managers are tasked with ensuring that the new employee is provided with the right guidance and tools to allow them to transition into their roles as seamlessly as possible.

Orientation programs or "onboarding" are a good start in teaching the employees the basics about the company after which the employee should be capable of demonstrating their understanding of the vision and brand of their employer. It is then that the true integration of corporate brand and personal image will take shape.

After appropriate training employees are accountable for their conduct and how they interact with others in their new environment and ideally will become model employees for that company and represent their brand with dignity and respect.

Without strong branding in place employees may resort to blindly establishing their own concept of the brand, much of which may not align with the company vision.

When there is such disconnection between the branding and the culture it could impact morale, productivity, and ultimately revenue. It is important for leadership within the company to establish their identity or how they want their customers, peers, and key stakeholders to know them. How can they do this? The easiest way would be to have everyone wear a uniform that incorporates the company logo like Apple or McDonald's does.

Imagine if Apple never mandated that all of their store employees wear the approachable logoed t-shirt and casual pants. You could walk into an Apple store and see some employees dressed in jeans and t-shirts and other employees wearing business attire with jackets and ties. What brand message would they be sending to their customers? Where is the reliability that all employees know the products and can serve you? Which employee would you prefer to assist you? This is why consistency is always a necessity when establishing a brand.

People are often approached with questions and comments when they are wearing a company logo. With every employee standing ready, armed with company information and prepared to answer questions about the company, branding awareness is heightened.

If a company becomes more focused on their bottom line, failing to tie culture to their brand or failing to realize the importance of establishing a brand that will distinguish them from the competition, they are missing the mark.

So what about global organizations? How is branding done when the company is a major investment bank or a pharmaceutical giant? These companies have thousands of employees worldwide in various functions and roles. It would be nearly impossible to have them all wear logoed clothing when their positions call for a more professional business look. This is when the vision and brand must be an integral part of each employee, who will in turn transcend this in everything they do as representatives for that company.

Using Image to Support Corporate Brand

Brand image is the sum total of all perceptions by a company's customers and signifies what the brand stands for.

Apple Founder, Steve Jobs, always presented an approachable persona by being casually dressed when he gave his presentations on Apple products. While that may have been his personal style he was at the same time representing the image branding of his Apple products. The company has imitated his example as we see store employees dressed casually meshing culture and product simplicity.

When you walk into the Apple Store, someone who is friendly, knowledgeable, willing to help, and who visually represents the Apple brand is there to greet you. You look around the store and see all employees dressed in the trademark blue t-shirts. They all seem to be free spirited techies and eager to assist you with your technical needs and challenges. This all sounds familiar, right? Your visual image of those employees is an extension of the Apple brand.

Apple is one of the world's most valuable brands. They have done a tremendous job of putting the customer experience at the center of everything they do. The enormity of Apple is evident as soon as you step in the door from the visible logo to having the employees poised to describe their brand as reliable, useful, and easy to approach. Based on these perceptions an image is formed and this is how Apple uses its employees, their attitudes and their appearance to carry its brand.

Microsoft, Apple's biggest competitor, has begun to follow

the Apple blueprint of integrating their company's image with their sales team. Now, when you walk into a Microsoft store you see knowledgeable sales people dressed in Microsoft brand t-shirts offering the same level of customer service as Apple.

I used the example of Apple and Microsoft to demonstrate how a company integrates their brand with the physical appearance of their workers. That was just one example; there are hundreds of companies that use this same strategy. Think about McDonalds, Burger King, Wendy's, or retailers like Best Buy. These companies all mandate that their employee's wear the company colors and logo.

What about cosmetic companies. Do you walk into a department store and see representatives from MAC and Bobbi Brown wearing attire that depicts their respective company's brand? Probably.

Regardless of your line of business or industry, the most productive companies are those that are able to bridge employee image to the company brand.

Now that I have discussed professional, business casual and dress-down attire and have given you an idea about how clothing helps with branding. ... let's delve into your Inner Image.

PART II
Inner Image

Inner image refers to those intrinsic characteristics that are ingrained within everyone. Confidence, self-esteem, and your inner drive or motivations all help shape your inner image.

There is a very fine line between confidence and arrogance; where as arrogance is usually a display of superiority or a false assumption that one can do something that he isn't really capable of doing, confidence is backed up by successful accomplishments.

In my discussion of inner image I will cover attitude, confidence and the importance of taking care of your physical health.

Attitude Is Everything

It's often said that your attitude makes the difference in just about everything that you set out to do in life. If you have a poor attitude it can affect your ability to start and complete those things you want to accomplish.

When I started writing this book I knew that I had to rid myself of any doubt or negative feelings in order to complete the project. I knew that if I listened to the negativity of a few about "how difficult it is to write a book" or "how challenging it is to get published," I might have tossed the idea of writing the book down the drain. There have been ideas from the past that I didn't complete because of other people's opinions. I have learned that only my opinion counts in regard to my life choices.

As an adult I always subscribe to positive thinking when faced with challenges. Whether it's personal, physical, professional, academic, or social in nature, having a positive outlook has always worked for me.

In 2006 I was diagnosed with cancer. I was told that the cancer had metastasized and that I would need chemotherapy to rid my body of cancerous cells. At the time, my daughter was 4 years old and I was in the prime of my professional career. Having lost both my parents and a host of relatives to this horrible disease was not encouraging and did not give me the best feeling, outlook or hope. The fact that they had all succumbed so early in their lives shook my confidence that I could fight or win this battle. Interestingly though, in the depth of my own crisis, I recalled that everyone that I lost to cancer had displayed a great deal of courage in the darkness of his or her struggle. I held on to that memory and it became the inspiration for the courage I needed in my own battle with cancer.

The cancer diagnosis could have signaled the end of my life and it would have been a disastrous outcome for my loving family so I am grateful today to be a cancer survivor and I tell everyone how much my faith and positive attitude helped me through the struggle. During that time I was reading "The Secret" by Rhonda Byrne (Byrne, 2007). The Secret gave me the extra motivation I needed to maintain a positive attitude. It helped me visualize my healing and envision my future with me living a wondrous life. By maintaining a positive attitude, summoning my courage and determination, and with efficient medical intervention I survived cancer and today I am thriving. I am so grateful to God for giving me another chance at life.

Everyone has their own methods for overcoming challenges, as there is no exact science because we are all different. What works for you may not work for me or vice versa. An underlying common denominator for winning and being successful is to be determined and deliberate in your actions. Being successful will truly depend on how you approach your life challenges.

What I can say with absolute assurance, however, is having a positive attitude is key. I had many difficult challenges with the medical, mental, and physical complexities of cancer and because I maintained a positive attitude and sought and followed the appropriate medical advice I was able to fight through that dire diagnosis.

This same attitude has been beneficial in my profession too. As someone who worked in sales for many years and had to interact with clients and other professionals with strong personalities, I found that keeping a healthy, positive attitude helped me stay focused and successful throughout my career.

As you work to *Discover Your Best Self*, your attitude will be the driving factor to success. Stay positive and focused on your goals and your potential for great results will follow!

Establishing And Building Confidence

Confidence comes from many factors. For some it is the type of initials after their name. For others it is the number of trophies in their trophy case or degrees on their wall. It could be the size of their house; the number of cars they have, the amount of money in their bank account, how proud they make their family ... the list goes on. What gives us confidence is usually something we have already done or achieved. Decide what you need to work on that will allow you to feel good about yourself. If that means losing weight or gaining weight ... work on it. Take those first steps and make it a part of your everyday routine. It may take you longer or shorter than average but keep focused and visualize your ultimate goal.

Don't be afraid to seek advice from experts or those who have reached the goals that you aspire to. There is no one better to learn from than someone who is successful in the same arena and your seeing that it can be accomplished will help build your confidence to move forward. Never shy away from asking for help. There is always someone willing to pay it forward, share his or her knowledge, and guide you. The key is to have faith, perseverance, and confidence. Be consistent as you work towards your goal.

My personal story is about my mother's desire to see me graduate from college. As I approached college age she made sure that I had the confidence, the will, and passion to want to go to college and succeed. I remember her staying up late with me as I worked towards my undergraduate degree. She would sit in our dining room as I studied for exams and she always let me know that she had unwavering confidence in me. My desire to make her proud is what drove me to succeed and I consistently made the Dean's List semester after semester. I would go on to obtain my Master's degree.

After my mother passed away, I continued to use what she had given me … desire and drive, and especially confidence to become a top performer in the highly competitive pharmaceuticals industry. I was one of the youngest professionals working for one of largest pharmaceutical companies and eventually became the number one representative in my district where I remained a top salesperson for several years.

Throughout my 20-year plus career, I worked in many different capacities holding many positions and several different titles and in each, I strove to be an outstanding performer. I remembered that my mother had set a standard of excellence and left me with the same fierce determination and courage that churned inside of her. Today as I look back, I am grateful for her as well as all the family members who were around me and helped to motivate me and build my confidence. It takes a team and a village to stand behind you as you make your way through the world and I always had my cheering section. However, I would be remiss if I did not concede that there were those who doubted me, but I worked tirelessly to prove them wrong! And I did.

The moral here is that we have to find out what motivates us, set goals, and then work towards achieving them. Each and every success will build your confidence and lead you to *Discover Your Best Self.*

Be Confident Not ... Arrogant

There is big difference between being confident and being arrogant. Arrogance is viewed in a negative light when used to describe a person's character. "Her arrogance was so apparent by her condescending tone and the way she alluded to knowing it all."

Arrogance doesn't win you friends or clients and can actually have a harmful impact on your career. Being arrogant is akin to thinking you know everything and that you are better than others and often with an offensive or overbearing attitude. Not how you want to be perceived!

Confidence, on the other hand, is a more positive attribute. "Her confidence was apparent by the way she addressed every question and demonstrated her command over the subject matter." Efficiency, and knowledge are elements that come with confidence and while confidence comes naturally to some it has to be developed by others.

You can develop confidence when you are learning a new skill or craft by consistent practice. Repetition is the mother of success. Initially your confidence may be hindered by your lack of experience doing something new but it will increase as you become more proficient in your skills. If having confidence can work for you, how does the lack of confidence work against you? Let me use driving as an example of what I mean.

I remember when I first learned to drive that there were certain roads that I did not want to drive on. Being inexperienced I was afraid of the larger vehicles, especially the 18-wheel tractor-trailers and buses that commanded the road. As long as I stayed off the roads where those 18-wheelers were I felt safe. But in time I came to realize it was limiting my mobility and that the lack of confidence in my own driving ability was making me miss out on pretty important events. I decided to put forth an intentional effort to overcome my fright.

The more I drove, almost instantly I started to gain more confidence in my ability. Of course I had a couple of minor "mishaps" but I didn't let that outweigh my desire to drive or be independent. I realized I needed to become a "road warrior" in order to get where I wanted to go and do the things I wanted to do. My desire outweighed my fear and my confidence began to overshadow my insecurities. I made up my mind that I could do it and I did! The secret, as I learned long ago while reading the book of the same name, is to visualize the outcome that you want and believe that you can accomplish it.

Later, the fact that I had chosen a career in Pharma continued to boost my driving confidence. I was required to be in my company car driving to see clients' every day, 5 days a week! I had no choice. It became mind over matter and I embraced driving in all types of weather conditions. I had to drive on highways, in big cities, at nighttime, in heavy traffic and on the roads with the big wheelers. Eventually I forgot about my initial fear of driving and all it had taken was practice.

You will build your confidence over time whether it's in driving, public speaking, sales, or in other professional skills with a concentrated and intentional effort. The more you practice, the better you will get. The better you get the more confident you'll become and the circle is complete.

I know so many people with all the right tools, skill sets, and abilities but I am constantly disappointed that they haven't succeeded or advanced the way they should. In most cases it's a lack of confidence. I know people with law degrees who doubt their ability to stand before a judge and competently represent their clients and others with medical degrees who do not actively practice medicine because of a lack of confidence in their skills. Know the phrase, "Use it or lose it?" It's true if you don't practice your craft.

You probably know people who "can't ... simply because they don't." Excuses like, "I can't drive on highways; I can't swim; I can't finish school" are all just that ... excuses. Don't let that be you. You control your own destiny but it's done with hard work, dedication, discipline, and determination.

Diet, Exercise, And Meditation

The road to enjoying a long, healthy, and happy life calls for us to discover what works for us physically that will also enhance our lives holistically. Certainly, exercise is on the list along with healthy diet as being beneficial in keeping one fit.

Some people who think diet is the most important factor to help one sustain a healthy life are meticulous about what they put into their bodies. Then there are the extreme opposite group of people who literally eat themselves into an early grave with careless and reckless abandon about what they put into their bodies.

Our eating habits have often been influenced by our culture, religion, and socioeconomic status so as adults we have to reevaluate how and what we eat and consider new ways of cooking.

When we are young our parents control our eating but as everyone reaches adolescence they gain more control over what they want to eat and that might be when weight struggles begin.

If weight is an issue for you, controlling it may be one of the single, most challenging things you face in life. Our individual body types and metabolism determines how fast we gain and or lose weight and not every diet or exercise plan will work for everyone. There are many ways to stay strong and healthy and literally hundreds if not thousands of different diet and exercise plans available to us all.

Find the system that is the right one and will work for you. That may mean joining a gym, hiring a personal trainer for a while, or working out at home. Some people can exercise on the fly and watch their caloric intake and be successful with weight control. Decide what you need to do and stick with it. Like with everything else in our lives, we have the ability to assess our personal situations, determine our plan of attack, and do what's best for us when it comes to maintaining a healthy mind, body, and soul.

Let's talk a bit about meditation. Meditation means having some quiet mental time to reflect and focus on things that are good for our soul and inner being. I personally try to make it a common daily practice to meditate and get in touch with my inner self and listen to what my higher power (God) is saying. I grew up with a solid spiritual foundation and meditation allows me to stay connected to God and to hear what he is telling me.

I've used meditation to help me sort out various challenges that I've encountered. Meditation allows you to clear your mind … similar to cleaning out a crowded closet.

Isn't it such a satisfying feeling to unpack or clear out a closet that has things that you no longer need while making room for those things that are important to you? Think of this in respect to accomplishing your life goals. Meditation can help you achieve balance, sorting out the useful from the useless. If you allow meditation to keep you focused and in tune with your desires, then you will be more likely to remain steadfast as you travel the road to your successes.

Harnessing the skill required to effectuate meditation requires that you set aside the time that works best for you and commit to it. This could be in the morning after you wake, during your commute to or from work, at lunchtime or whenever you can find the opportunity to unpack mentally.

The great thing about meditating is that all it requires is time. That time can be as short or as long as you want it to be. You can determine where and when you meditate and it doesn't always have to be in the same place. You don't have to worry about whether you have equipment, the right shoes, or the right outfit for meditation. Meditate as often as you see fit to do so. Your success lies in knowing how to use meditation to channel positive energy to get you through challenging moments.

Road To Success

Success, as we have talked about it, isn't an obscure, secret technique that only a few can access but it does require your desire and effort.

Don't fall into the habit of giving up too easily. "If at first you don't succeed ... try, try again. Persistence pays off in the end.

Dedicate yourself to practicing the principals in this book: etiquette, proper dress, confidence, attitude and establishing strong outward and inward images, and you will be at the doorstep to success.

Treat yourself with the same desire for perfection that you extend to others. Always present your best image whether you are in your work environment, at school with your peers, or among family and friends at a social gathering. Be your best self.

Think of it in this way: If you were a master homebuilder you would use tools that allow you to build the best home for your customer, right? You would want to erect a masterpiece because it would be a reflection of your skills and a representation of your abilities. Build yourself in the same manner. You are deserving of the best.

Now, I will discuss how to create a winning mindset and how understanding yourself and all your personality nuances will strengthen you on your path to self-discovery.

Create A Winning Mindset

We should create and establish a winning mindset in everything that we do and I use the book written by the late Dr. Stephen Covey, *The 7 Habits of Highly Effective People* (Covey, 1989) to help me do that.

Begin With The End In Mind; Put First Things First; Think Win-Win." Those are 3 of *The 7 Habits of Highly Effective People.* I am a longtime proponent of Dr. Covey and his advice that there is a specific pathway for living with integrity and human dignity, fairness and service. His book is essentially a manual on how to balance personal and professional effectiveness. I try to employ these habits in my daily life along with the other four: "Seek First to Understand, Then to be Understood," "Be Proactive," "Synergize," and "Sharpen the Saw."

Dr. Covey, said that highly effective people should "sharpen the saw," meaning practice their skill. The first habit of highly effective people is proactivity. Proactive people are driven. Don't allow yourself to fall behind or waste a talent because it requires you to be diligent. Put in the time needed to perfect it.

Covey spoke of Character Ethic, where one's success is attributed to underlying characteristics such as integrity, courage, and patience. Combine character ethics with personality traits like a positive attitude and you will be on the road to success. Challenge yourself to build the confidence that will take you to higher heights in your career or in your personal life. Don't allow anyone to tell you what you can or cannot do. Be confident that with consistent practice, you can be at the top of your game in whatever you choose to do.

I am careful to always plan my steps, which holds me accountable for my actions. It will serve you well to understand the concepts of Dr. Covey's book and his belief of what the foundation of success is. Try implementing these 7 steps in your daily life.

Over the years I've had many leadership roles in various organizations. As a result I've had the opportunity to learn about several leadership styles and a multitude of techniques as it pertains to being an effective leader. Being enlightened by some of the most sought after thought leaders has helped me discover my best self in many ways. Jim Collins' *Good to Great* has been a reference point for me. According to Collins *"Leading from good to great does not mean coming up with the answers and then motivating everyone to follow your messianic vision. It means having the humility to grasp the fact that you do not yet understand enough to have the answers and then to ask the questions that will lead to the best possible insights."*

"*Having the humility*" … this is such an important aspect to leadership. I have found that the best leaders embrace this characteristic. Humility allows you to accept the fact that you may not have all of the answers or solutions to make you the best in your field; but you are willing to listen and observe those who can help you get to the pinnacle point that you desire.

Some major corporations have had to "Discover their Best Selves" as they re-strategized their business plans. In his book, Collins mentions how Wells Fargo, attempting to become a global player in the banking industry, had to discover what they were best at. With that discovery Wells Fargo went on to become one of the best performing banks in the financial service industry.

First, Set Smart Goals

Set a goal that is attainable. In the pharmaceutical industry setting "SMART" goals was a part of my annual responsibility. SMART goals are Specific, Measurable, Attainable, Realistic, and Timely. By setting SMART goals we give ourselves a realistic road to success and achievability. Let's discuss what SMART goals are all about and how this can help us develop a winning mindset.

Be "Specific" in what it is you want to accomplish. If you want to obtain a degree then you know that your goal is academic. If you want to lose or gain weight, then your goal is targeted around physical fitness or your diet. Be precise in determining the area of your life that your goal focuses on and stick to whatever it is you need to do. Specificity is key!

Measure it! Next, determine how you will chart your progress. What will allow you to track and measure how close you are to meeting that goal? If it's weight loss, you can monitor your weight weekly or at a frequency that allows you to see how close you are to your target weight. Whatever the goal, find a way to be accountable so that you stay on track.

Attainable. Let's be clear, your goals have to be attainable. Will it be possible for you to do what you are setting out to do? Does it require more than you are willing to give? If your goal is to graduate with a degree from a 4-year college, you can't do it if you drop out of school. If you want to buy a house, don't think you can do it without saving money for a down payment. If you keep it real with yourself, attainability is possible.

Be Realistic. Don't set yourself up for failure by setting the goal too high. Is it possible to obtain, acquire or accomplish the goal? If it is so out of your reach, then you need to reexamine and reevaluate. We'd like to think we could lose 20 pounds in a week, but really?

The last SMART goal is "Timely" and to accomplish your goals you will need to set a time in which you intend to reach completion. Be reasonable, Rome wasn't built in a day.

There is no easy road to success. Unfortunately. The road is usually not straight but instead winds, curves, and twists. Sometimes it's a hard and complicated journey but it's well worth the trip. To avoid the work brings the most difficulty. Don't fight success; embrace the challenge.

"The early bird gets the worm." We all know the story of the early bird who arrives first and as a result has the best chance of success. Then there is the fable about *The Ant and The Grasshopper* wherein the hungry grasshopper begs for food from an ant when winter comes and he finds himself without food. The ant refuses. The lesson extols the virtues of hard work and planning for the future. In short, put in the hard work today so that you can be better off in the future. Set SMART goals. Sure, you can dream and I never want you to limit your dreams but keep in mind ... there is a difference between a dreamer and a realist. You will appreciate the fruits of your labor knowing that you earned them through your own efforts and not on someone's coattails.

Here is a table that provides a list of goals and an example of how to provide a SMART Road Map to accomplish those goals:

Goal	"SMART" ROAD MAP				
	Specific	Measurable	Attainable	Realistic	Timely
Weight Loss	My goal is physical fitness and healthy weight loss.	I will chart my progress by weighing in weekly.	I can lose 10 lbs. in 30 days if I manage my diet and exercise at least 10 to 20 minutes 3 times per week.	10 lbs. in 30 days.	I will determine my progress in 1 month
4 Year College Degree	I want to get a degree to give me more options.	I need to complete a certain amount of credits each semester.	I can accomplish this goal by completing the required credits in 4 years.	As long as I stay in school I will accomplish this goal.	At the end of my 4-year program I will have my degree.
Career Promotion	I want to get promoted to the next level in my career path.	I should be promoted within 2 years.	The current position I am in has a structured career path	Every step in the career path is attainable.	If I meet all the requirements I should be promoted within the specified time period for promotions.

Emotional Intelligence (EI)

It is important that I discuss Emotional Intelligence, its five components and how it enhances our own professional growth.

Daniel Goleman, Ph.D., a science journalist, and author of the New York Times bestseller *Emotional Intelligence and Social Intelligence: The New Science of Human Relationships*, developed the following five key components of EI:

1. Self-Awareness (recognizing your own moods and emotions and their effect on others).

2. Self-Regulation (think before acting).

3. Internal Motivation (optimism and inner vision).

4. Empathy (understanding the emotional makeup of other people).

5. Social Skills (managing relationships; finding common ground).

One of the benefits of Emotional Intelligence is that it allows us to control our own emotions, the emotions of others and to identify, distinguish and give a name to feelings and hence use that emotional information to redirect thinking and behavior to achieve our goals.

In pharmaceutical sales, I worked in and around various facilities where people with different diseases were being treated. Each day I went to a different facility promoting and selling my company's products. My job, ideally, was to help save the lives of those living with potentially debilitating and fatal illnesses. Under those circumstances my ability to be empathetic, to be self-aware and to use my social skills were a necessity in order to be successful and effective.

In dealing with clients I found that it required my own self-regulation as I went about my job. My company would oftentimes put policy changes in place without notice and I had very demanding clientele who were not necessarily understanding of that. Some of these changes would affect my ability to provide benefits that had been previously extended to them. For example, a policy change may have impacted the amount of compensation a speaker was paid at a dinner program. While not my fault, I was placed in the position to bare the burden of a client's verbal displeasure about those changes and how it hurt their financial bottom line and ability to make money. My capacity to understand the emotions of those I interacted with daily was a key component to my EI. I understood the client's concern and listened with sincerity despite my lack of power to change policy. Communication and interaction are the training grounds for EI.

As you *Discover Your Best Self* you must be able to manage your emotional intelligence. The greatest leaders master this skill. Steve Jobs of Apple was a great leader who knew what his customers wanted and set out at all cost to provide them with the best technology available. His EI, empathy, and social skills allowed him to understand his customers and he realized that making simple and reliable devices would satisfy consumers. Today, Apple provides customers with unparalleled service. This simple concept translated into billions of dollars in earnings for Apple.

Self-Awareness

Self-awareness involves being aware of your internal and external environment. It is your ability to recognize and understand your personal moods, emotions and drives. One who exercises sound self-awareness is often able to discern a situation proactively rather than reactively. Case in point: Someone who analyzes the environment before making blanket statements that could be seen as offensive to others is exercising self-awareness. Case in point: In HIV clinics there were situations when I walked into a roomful of patients receiving treatment for their illnesses. Some of these clinics were not the best looking facilities and were often located in less fortunate, inner city neighborhoods. In these surroundings it might not have been uncommon for someone to be a little uneasy and unintentionally react in an offensive manner.

Being self-aware of how my own moods or emotions could be interpreted by those patients undergoing treatment reminded me to consciously show sensitivity and respect. I made a concerted effort to be friendly and sympathetic yet respect their privacy and help them maintain their dignity. In the same scenario, someone lacking emotional intelligence might react in an offensive manner by not wanting to touch something they perceive as contaminated or sit where someone who was sick had just vacated. An insensitive person might even make facial expressions if a patient were to sneeze or cough in their presence. Body language can be an indicator that one is uncomfortable and can inadvertently send signals that insult a patient. Visually showing your negative emotions may create an awkward atmosphere for everyone in the room so try and be mindful in situations like that.

Self-Regulation

Self-regulation allows us to have control over our immediate and disruptive impulses without intervention from external forces. When you self regulate you equip yourself with the ability to monitor and control your behavior, impulses, and thoughts … adjusting them accordingly with the situation.

It takes willpower and self-control to self regulate when it come to attaining some of your goals. For example, if you decide that you need to lose weight, then you must follow the diet explicitly and not give in to eating the foods you'd really like to eat.

Self-regulation allows you to act in your long-term best interest because you take the time to consider all possibilities. Someone who self-regulates monitors their own behavior while those who do not will react without thinking about the consequence of those actions.

When you self regulate you develop the skill to cheer yourself up when you're down, or calm your self down when you're upset. Lack of self-regulation can lead to irrational decision-making and hinder your ability to reach your goals.

Internal Motivation

Internal motivation is that motor that propels us to work towards our goals. It is the desire to accomplish something that has been ignited by our personal internal aspiration or generated by a burning passion to do, give or be. It is doing an action because you enjoy it.

One may say that it is the sheer internal motivation of a philanthropist to donate time, endless amounts of money and personal sacrifice to those causes they have deemed important and are dedicated to help. Professional athletes who play for the "love of the game" oftentimes have internal motivation that allows them to persevere and not fail or quit. To become a prominent physician, well-respected lawyer, or any type of professional requires tireless dedication, vision and optimism that your goals are achievable.

Internal motivation is the answer to the "what and why" one does what they do. It's why they don't want to stop learning, practicing or striving. There are two types of internal motivation: one comes from direct enjoyment of engaging in a given task (intrinsic) and the other comes from a sense of internalized obligation or responsibility to engage in a task (extrinsic). Harness your intrinsic motivation, that which you are driven to do, even if there is no reward or compensation and it will speed you on your way to success and fulfillment.

Empathy

Empathy is often said to be the cornerstone to emotional intelligence. To be empathetic requires you to have perspective and balance and to be able to see things from others viewpoint. Someone with tunnel vision, (narrow-mindedness, single-mindedness or close-mindedness) may be inhibited from showing empathy simply because they cannot put themselves in another's shoes and are unable to relate to the plight of others.

Empathy is often confused with sympathy. While empathy equates to sharing and understanding the emotional makeup of others, sympathy means feelings of sorrow or pity for someone else's misfortune. Empathy is insight, compassion, appreciation, and recognition as opposed to pity, which often has condescending overtones.

A person who lives in a privileged environment all of their lives and are used to having everything they need and desire at their fingertips may not be able to understand or relate to someone who lives day-to-day, wondering how he or she will make it from moment to moment. A less compassionate person might argue that those who are faced with hardship, particularly financial hardships, brought much of those problems on themselves perhaps by their lack of initiative or drive to succeed.

Instead of shaking your fingers in shame at those living in dire conditions or facing insurmountable daily difficulties why not lend a helping hand? Their situation could be due to a myriad of reasons including the mismanagement of their finances, mismanagement of people or mismanagement of themselves. We have to be able to empathize with those facing economic hardships the same way that we would empathize with someone with a physical ailment caused by sickness or an accident. By being empathetic we are raising our EI to a level that will allow us to better understand various situations, people and cultures. Develop empathy and you will *Discover Your Best Self.*

Social Skills

As I write this I am thinking of the numerous ways that information is gathered, disseminated and communicated today. It has impacted and changed how we correspond with one another.

Social media has made it possible for us to connect by simply touching an icon on our smart devices. We no longer have to pick up the phone for verbal conversation, instead we text or tweet. I remember always wondering why telephones had letters under the numbers; now I know it's because the universe knew that texting would one day be used more often than calling! Have you ever noticed a group of teenagers who sit at a table together with their smart phones in hand and instead of engaging in live conversation are busy texting, sending pictures and watching videos?

What are some of the drawbacks of using texting and tweeting more than participating in live communication? Are our social skills being compromised? I would say yes. Failing to connect with one another, create conversation or have verbal discussions weakens social skill growth.

Social skills involve managing relationships and finding common ground. Having sufficient and adequate social abilities supports your capacity to communicate, persuade and interact with others without creating unnecessary conflict or tension. Adequate social skills enable people to get along. It is much easier to hide behind a text, tweet or anonymous comment than to stand front and center and present your point of view, state your case, or defend the your opinion. To speak up or speak out calls for mature social skills.

The ability to communicate in a social setting empowers us to be more self-aware, more empathetic and allows us to self-regulate any disruptive emotions we might feel in a heated debate.

Those who have outstanding social skills are often seen as the life of the party. They engage others in conversation and move among the partygoers with ease. They have a wide array of views and welcome the interaction and connection with others through verbal stimulation.

Hearing others point of view can increase your own appreciation and awareness about certain facts of life. Conversation becomes food for thought and allows you to build empathy for the experiences of those who may not have a choice in matters that affect their lives. So how do we develop these skills? Become social!

Realistically, opening up and taking yourself out of your comfort zone to increase your sociability is easier said than done for some of us, but work on it as you work on *Discovering Your Best Self.*

Having dissected the components of Emotional Intelligence, there are two additional qualities and character traits I want to mention, that are equally as important on your road to self-discovery.

Humility

"Never forget where you came from." Those are words that I often heard from my parents when I was a child. As we accomplish our goals and achievements, humility is humbleness and is what keeps us from changing and becoming consumed by our successes. It keeps us balanced and provides us with a holistic perspective on life.

How often do we see individuals who reach the pinnacle of their careers, only to fall hard because they became consumed and overwhelmed by the material successes they achieved?

When you've reached the top or when you've "arrived" it is easy to lose focus and begin to believe the "hype." You become a victim of your own success because you now equate your self-worth to the material things that you've gotten.

Keep things in perspective. Always remember where you started and stay true to yourself. Remember your efforts, the countless hours and the number of times it may have taken you to achieve your goals. Appreciate and respect success. Teach others the importance of hard work.

Lack of humility causes us to turn our backs on our past as we begin to over evaluate our own importance and it is often responsible for our failure to reach back and help those less fortunate.

Be kind to those who are not where you are, as they may not have had the same resources and opportunities. We find people living below the poverty line because perhaps they lost their jobs or were victims of betrayal or deceitfulness that cost them their life savings. Never judge anyone by his or her appearance and remember, "But for the grace of God, go I." When you encounter someone who needs it, give them hope and encouragement.

Let your conscience be your guide. Allow your humility to keep you grounded in positive values that will provide those around you with the encouragement and inspiration they need to hurdle the obstacles in their lives and accomplish their goals.

I belong to several organizations that provide services to the homeless and underprivileged and on a monthly basis we provide hot meals to those in need. The time we spend preparing for these events does not come close to the enormous gratitude and appreciation that we receive in return. Serving others allows us to put things in the proper perspective and while we've worked hard to acquire our "material things" we must also remember to be appreciative of what we have and take nothing for granted.

Stay humble at every step in life. Humility or modesty is what keeps us true and honest and allows us to stay rooted and grounded in the beliefs that were instilled in us as children.

Self-Reflection

Self-reflection, according to the English Oxford dictionary is *meditation or serious thought about one's character, actions, and motives*. Webster defines self-reflection as *self-examination*. As you work towards knowing yourself it is important that you examine your emotional self. This is essential and if done correctly and honestly, it will allow you to identify your strengths and weaknesses.

In graduate school, depending on the project, we often performed what is known as a *SWOT Analysis*. We were tasked with identifying *Strengths, Weaknesses, Opportunities and Threats.*

I believe that human self-reflection is the capacity to exercise introspection along with the willingness to learn more about our fundamental purpose and nature so that we can perform a SWOT analysis of our own character, actions and motives.

When I started college I had already decided on pursuing my degree in marketing. I knew that marketing would be the path to a career where I could afford the lifestyle I envisioned. As graduation drew close I identified the pharmaceutical industry as the area of focus for achieving my personal goals. I identified the skill set needed and knew I would have to work on some of my internal shortcomings to be successful.

I landed my first job and after weeks of intensive training, I was certain that I had developed the skills necessary for the position. . It turns out those skills would be tested often as I had to present technical data to medical professionals on a reoccurring basis. These professionals interacted with hundreds of territory business managers weekly and expected a certain level of professionalism and knowledge. Needless to say my entry road was not without a few bumps.

I was a novice to many of the presentation tools and computer software applications that I needed to drive home my company message and secure the sale. Convincing the customer or client that my company's prescribed solution was their best option was my job so I had to step up my game. Sometimes you don't know everything you think you know but realizing this is a step up the ladder to a better you.

I immediately enrolled myself in classes focused on how to use Microsoft PowerPoint, Word and Excel. This additional schooling helped me to strengthen my presentations and I immediately began to secure more sales. I put forth a lot of effort to develop my skills and be competitive and my commitment to learn and be successful eventually took me to the top but it had taken a conscious endeavor requiring a time commitment and strong constitution.

A part of being self-reflective means doing the work to make yourself the best that you can be. During your self-reflective/ self-examination process, determine what you are good at and enhance those skills instead of doing a mediocre job with skills that require a bit more practice to achieve competency.

Talent comes in degrees and levels. We hear athletes talk about how much time they spend in the gym, on the tennis court, or in the batting cages to assure that they will be the best in their field. Some skill and abilities come easily to some while others have to work harder. We can certainly concede that there are those with natural, God given talents who do not need as much practice as the average athlete to be a star. Nevertheless, the vast majority of even the best athletes spend a lot of time perfecting their skills. A few exceptional players who separated themselves from their peers by their work ethic: Michael Jordan, Gabby Douglas, Michael Phelps, Serena Williams ... the list can go on. They will tell you about the countless hours spent sharpening their talent. They are also self-reflective. He is a tremendous Olympic swimmer and loves having a gold medal around his neck, but you will probably never see Michael Phelps in a tryout for the New York Yankees. Knowing the limitations of your talents and your skills come from your ability to self-reflect.

Self-Empowerment

I remember Reading Is Fundamental (RIF) when I was growing up. RIF is a literacy organization committed to inspiring reading passion among children.

Those three letters resonated in my thoughts throughout my grammar school days and carried me through college and graduate school. I always believed that education should be ongoing and was the key to being empowered. "You're never too old to learn" and "You learn something new every day" are true sayings. I encourage you to expand your mind by learning something new every day and never stop getting and absorbing as much information as possible. While formal education and securing the best academic experience possible is the route for some, I do want to make one thing clear: It's not for everyone and it's not the only way.

Self-empowerment does not necessarily mean getting a degree or becoming a licensed professional. Self-empowerment can mean doing whatever it is that you believe is best for you; understanding your strengths and weaknesses along with knowing your limitations. It gives you the ability to take control of your life and take the steps to set and achieve goals. Be creative in the ways that you can obtain your goals; don't limit yourself. Think outside the box. Shift your paradigm. Expand your horizons.

You may read a 500-page novel or a 5-paragraph article and that knowledge can be self empowering. It might be the quality of the content you read and not necessarily the quantity. You can spend 15 minutes walking on a treadmill and feel as good as if you spent 50 minutes running. Your sense of accomplishment is only limited by the goals you set ... not the goals that others set for you.

Your best self is waiting to be discovered. The key is to always set realistic goals and find the formula that works for you in all aspects of your life. While nothing in life is impossible, be true to yourself and don't set your standards abnormally high. Set accurate goals so that you don't sabotage yourself. This is an example of an unrealistic goal: A 300lb. samurai wrestler who aspires to beat a world-class sprinter in the 100-meter dash. This is very unlikely and almost laughable to imagine. What is he thinking? He could never out run a sprinter could he? Unrealistic to say the least! But stranger things have happened and the misfortune of a pulled hamstring at the start of the race could leave an opening for the samurai wrestler to win!

I hope that this overview of Creating a Winning Mindset along with the outlining a plan to work towards developing the 5 components of Emotional Intelligence will enrich your life. It will be through your own initiative that you reach your goals.

Discover Your Best Self

Whether it is etiquette, attitude, fashion faux pas, posture, or confidence, I wanted to provide important guides throughout this book to help you along the way to *Discover Your Best Self.*

I have covered a wide selection of subjects ranging from personal and corporate image to both inward and outward image. Be mindful that these are only suggestions. While confidence is primary, we also have to be open minded enough to discern what is in our best interests and what is not. It is essential to have the self-awareness to recognize our image and character flaws and the humility to undertake the work to become a better person.

I have discussed self-reflection and knowing your strengths

and your weaknesses. Never depending on anyone to validate my self-worth or determine my fate in life is a rule that I've applied since I was an adolescent. My mother instilled in me those values that allowed me to develop the confidence I needed on life's journey. It is my hope that through this book I have helped you uncover your own inner strength and desire to succeed.

It's an old, but true cliché ... "Keep your eyes on the prize" and never be deterred by failure but use negative outcomes as motivation to accomplish your goals. Doing so and standing strong in the face of disappointments are indicators that you have learned to appreciate and master your life. Take pride in every accomplishment you achieve no matter how small it may appear as it increases your confidence and encourages you to continue to work tenaciously through all barriers you encounter.

To *Discover Your Best Self* can be finding the exercise, diet, and lifestyle that you can maintain regularly without causing any strain to your mental or physical health. A healthy body breeds a healthy mind just as a healthy mind breeds a healthy body. The ability to focus and see the bigger picture and understand what works for you as well as discovering what systems will lead to your self-improvement and personal well being are key.

Uncovering your best self involves being able to establish, maintain, and nurture relationships that contribute to a positive attitude and outlook. Reading and watching content that enhances your emotions instead of creating doubt and pessimism is productive. Those materials will nourish your soul and fill you with positivity and hope. Putting the things that have the biggest impact in your life at the forefront and being able to understand and recognize what is holding you down will lead toward fulfillment. Your best self will always finish stronger than you started.

Being the best representation of yourself calls for the ability to show empathy for those facing situations that you cannot relate to and sharing your time and resources with those who need life's basic essentials is a generous and humbling experience. Working in a shelter on your off days or offering to provide a meal to those in need speaks to your character and your ability to connect with others.

Actually, taking time to purposely step out of your comfort zone to experience something that you've never experienced or to help someone in need says that you have discovered a desire to become your better self. Reach back and help those who may be in need of conversation, mentoring, guidance, encouragement, or career focus. Make yourself available to sincerely help an individual or take up a cause focused on improving the lives of others. Making a deposit into someone's emotional bank account (Covey, 1989) and doing something for someone out of the pure goodness of your heart with no expected compensation other than the satisfaction of the betterment of that person all are indicators that the best you has arrived.

Discover Your Best Self in every aspect of your life. Sharpen your saw; bring your A-game every day and be prepared for whatever life throws at you. Channel and harness courage from those whom you've seen fight the good fight and while they may have lost their battles here in the physical world, if you believe that they are winners in the spiritual realm, then that too, is a source of comfort as you move through your life. Always be grateful for the little things. Work hard, but smart and never forget to remain humble as you accrue material profits and rise up the ladder. Be resilient regardless of the circumstance; there is only one way to go if you're at the bottom ... up!

· *Discover Your Best Self,* I hope, will motivate you to take action to do more, be better, and to push harder. Don't allow someone to tell you that you can't. Instead use their doubt to ignite your determination to accomplish your life dreams and ambitions. Know yourself and recognize those people who will allow you to flourish and not stand in the way of or prevent your growth.

Build meaningful relationships and maintain those relationships by staying true to who you are instead of trying to be someone that you're not. Keeping in tune with your spirituality and your higher power and being able to find the quiet space to mentally unpack your thoughts and reevaluate your path will be immensely helpful on your personal road to discovery. Take time to meditate and get in touch with your inner self to relieve stress or anxiety and to gain a better understanding of your purpose.

Discover Your Best Self means celebrating life to the fullest and bringing those around you along for the ride. Always be aware that if there are no bumps on the path you are traveling ... you may be wandering down the wrong road. Reassess. Reevaluate. Recalculate. How you manage those bumps on your passage to fulfilling your life purpose is crucial and will say a lot about your constitution.

With this information and the guidelines I've provided about how to monitor your steps in life, realize your potential, and work with steadfast determination you are now well equipped for success.

I challenge you to *"Discover Your Best Self."* Yearn to be all that you can be. Use these tools to enhance the path or journey that is yours and yours alone. Take what works for you, implement it … and Yes, Stick with it!

Goleman's Model for Emotional Intelligence

Self -Awareness	Social Awareness
1. Emotional self-awareness	1. Empathy
2. Accurate Self-Assessment	2. Organizational Awareness
3. Self-Confidence	3. Service Orientation
Self Management	Relationship Management
1. Self Control	1. Inspirational Leadership
2. Transparency	2. Developing Others
3. Adaptability	3. Influence
4. Achievement Drive	4. Change Catalyst
5. Initiative	5. Conflict Management
	6. Building Bonds
	7. Teamwork & Collaboration

REFERENCES

Byrne, R., (2007). The Secret. Atria Books.

Collins, J. (2001). Good to Great. HarperCollins Publishing, Inc.

Covey, S. (1989). The Seven Habits of Highly Effective People. New York: Simon and Schuster.

Goleman, D. (2017) Emotional Intelligence. www.google.com/imgres?imgurl=https://web.sonoma.edu/users/s/swijtink/teaching/philosophy

Connect with Discover Your Best Self

www.discoveryourbestself.net

@DYBSconsulting

Hashtag

#discoveryourbestself

CPSIA information can be obtained
at www.ICGtesting.com
Printed in the USA
FFHW011135190519
52543712-58008FF

9 781480 864092